SALES TIPS YOU CAN BANK ON

BY

TODD STEPHEN HUNTER

authorHOUSE®

AuthorHouse™
1663 Liberty Drive, Suite 200
Bloomington, IN 47403
www.authorhouse.com
Phone: 1-800-839-8640

First published by AuthorHouse 12/12/2008

ISBN: 978-1-4389-1770-2 (sc)

Printed in the United States of America
Bloomington, Indiana

This book is printed on acid-free paper.

Nothing in my life has ever come without the assistance of others or a higher power. I express my gratitude to my Father, Steve, who if it were not for him I would not be in banking. I express my gratitude to my Mother, Sandy, for her passion for selling. My thanks go out to my clients who have stayed with me and have helped me along the way. This book would not have been possible if it were not for the inspiration of Mary Field my long time friend and her love for reading.

Contents

WHY CLIENTS BANK
WHERE THEY BANK

The answer to this question is found in the relationships between the client and the banker. In every area or demographic you will find a prospect saying to you, "I bank with xyz bank because they make banking so easy!" That brings me to the next point. How is it made so easy? The answer is that you as a banker have gained the client's trust and he or she feels comfortable with you handling his or her money. How many times have you heard people say they gave money to someone and that person lost it? Your job as a relationship banker is to make sure they have a safe place to keep their money where it will grow and provide a secure financial future for them.

Customer service is another reason why customers bank with you. Let me illustrate a few examples. One of my clients I have known for about four years from another financial institution. Just the other day he called me as he was on his way to the city. The payroll company screwed up his payroll. The payroll was supposed to be deposited the next business morning, but it wasn't going to happen. I suggested that he take money from his business account with us and make an official check. Since I know my client, I had an official check made and hand delivered it to where his other business account was. The next day the funds were available for use, and his employees were paid. The client could not believe that I would do that for him. These little things will make you first class as a banker.

A few months ago one of my clients in the mortgage industry whom I have known for the last couple of years needed me to do something for him. This may seem odd to you, but this particular client has never stepped foot in any of the branches that I have worked at. He asked me to make a draw off of his business line so he could bring some money to a real estate closing that afternoon. The closest branch to him was a half hour away. The closing was the very next morning from the time that he called me. I said to him, "I will have a check made and bring it to you for your closing." He said, "That would be great. Can you meet me at a restaurant at eight this evening and hand it to me?" That night I drove an hour to give my client his check. That night I was able to deepen the relationship even further.

On occasion I am one of the closing bankers. One night I noticed a car parked outside for an unusual amount of time to the point that it almost seemed suspicious. A few moments later another car arrived. A gentleman got out of the second car and began changing a young lady's car tire. The temperature that evening was around eight degrees. It was in the dead of winter here in Chicago. Our competition had closed for the day, and it was dark out. I glanced over at the coffee station and thought, *Why we don't bring two cups of coffee out to these people to keep them warm?* I went outside to offer them the coffee to keep them warm. In addition, we offered them to come inside if they needed to keep warm. About fifteen minutes later, the young lady came inside and chatted with us for a little while. I asked her about her car, employment, and of course, where she banks. As a result, I was able to set up an appointment to meet with her to talk about her banking needs. However, most importantly, when she passes by our bank she will remember what happened that cold night. People cared about some stranger in their parking lot and offered them to come inside. A month later I was able to do an onsite and sign up more than half of the employees to switch over to the bank that I work for.

All of these stories illustrate how you can separate yourself from the competition. Do you think the young lady with the flat tire and coffee in her hand cared about our current cd special?

The answer is probably not. When you ask your customers for a referral it will be no problem, because they trust you as their banker. People will bank where they have a relationship with someone. They will follow you when you do what is right for them and go the extra mile. They know that when they call you, you will call them back. They know when they have a problem you will not transfer them to five different departments. Clients don't care what your corporate structure is like or your policies. They called you for a reason—because you will take care of them.

Generally speaking customers don't want to feel like another number. When you think of how many banks and customers are out there, it is truly mind blowing. It is very easy for customers to feel like they are not important to the banker or the bank. When meeting customers for the first time, greet them with a smile and let them know you will be taking care of them. Use their names often during the first visit and the meetings to follow. Ask them when their kids' birthdays are and write them down, along with any other special events. Even take notes about what you discussed. When you meet with your client the next time, you will be able to bring up key information, whether it is business or personal. Regardless, they will know that you truly listened and care about their business and them as a person. Please don't be a banker who pushes product when a client sits down at your desk. This type of selling will not separate you from the rest of the competition. Get to know your clients. If they own a business, talk to them about their business. This is their passion that they created from scratch. Offer to send them referrals to patronize their business. Use the law of reciprocation, which means you need to give in order to receive. At some Indian trading posts, the patrons will shop and before they leave, the store clerk will give them a free token of appreciation. The same applies in banking. Find something that you can offer to your client as a small token of appreciation. Some may say I have given them an excellent rate. That's great, but so can some of the competition. Some ideas that you can give away may include coffee, soda, gift cards, and candy or bank promotional items. You can never give too much to a customer. By doing this you not only create brand loyalty, but it is also the beginning of a loyal client relationship. When you give them something, they will give you business back.

Time after time there are clients who bank at a certain place because of a person who works there. The bank's rates could be average. When you think of it, poor customer service is usually the reason clients will leave their bank and go to the competition. They come to you hoping that you can make their experience better. Be sure to ask them what they didn't like about their previous bank. It just like dating; you may want to know what annoys the other person before you dive in. Assure them that you will make sure that those things will not happen where they will bank now.

Sometimes people will choose a bank out of habit because maybe their family banks there. Sometimes they will bank at a particular bank because they are in the armed services and receive special rates on savings and loans. For business clients, they need a bank that can communicate on a regular basis. Their needs are more sophisticated and demanding than the consumer needs. People may choose a particular bank because it's convenient and they can shop where they bank as well. Certain clients may like the convenience of the online banking and other products that are being provided. Some clients may like the convenience of the hours the bank has to offer. Some may like the special senior citizen types of checking and savings accounts. Some may have the outlook that their bank will always give them what they need.

You see, when you do the things that no one else will do, your clients notice this, and they recognize you as being different than the competition. Guess what? Pretty soon there will not be any because you will have become so distant from what the competition does. Sometimes going out of the way for your clients may not be comfortable or convenient. That is perfectly okay, because being number one is not meant to be comfortable. It is similar to when I would drive an hour to see my top client, Vik Sagar at QDI Financial. He never set foot in any of the banks that I worked at, yet he chooses the bank where I work because I make it so convenient and give him the service that he needs. When you make these kinds of sacrifices on your clients' behalf, I know that relationship will be nourished and developed. People buy from people they have chemistry with who are always there for them, even after the sale is made. Why have your clients banked with you, or why will they bank with you? What can you offer them that is different from the competition?

How Well Do You Know Your Clients?

Today I had the opportunity to help an existing client convert his home equity line of credit to a home equity loan. He came into the bank with his son and sat in my office for about twenty minutes. While on hold with the lending department attempting to convert and lock in his interest rate, I began to have conversation with him, none of which had to do with banking. On his jacket was a logo of a silver airplane flying over a small city. I asked him what he did for a living out of curiosity. He told me that he is a private pilot and flies CEOs of companies around the world for business. His career, to me, seemed very rewarding in the sense that he probably learns a lot of different concepts while flying these executives back and forth. He then began to share with me how the company was founded and who started the company. I brought up questions about how many employees work there. How often does the company finance new airplanes? After this conversation of small talk, I asked permission to call the owner of the company to set an appointment to meet with him. He replied that would be fine. Always ask for referrals! The question could be as simple as, "Who of your family or friends is currently dissatisfied with their bank?"

A few weeks after talking to a client by the teller line, a client came in and began speaking to one of the tellers. He appeared as if he had just finished lifting weights and looked exhausted. After listening to the conversation at the teller line, I walked over and began to offer my assistance. But first his gold chain caught my attention and I inquired about it. I came to the conclusion that he was a weight lifter. I then invited him into my office and he told me that he owns a weight lifting business and has traveled extensively all over the country training athletes. I found his insight and business to be fascinating. I then started to help him with his business concerns. His problem was on his commercial mortgage. After a few minutes we were able to solve his issues together. Then a few questions later I found out that his sister owns a small boutique in town. His sister was in need of extra working capital and had a certificate of deposit coming due and was looking for a new bank. I asked him if it would be okay to give his sister a call and he said yes. Later on that day I gave his sister a call and set up a time for her to come in and talk about her financial needs. If one asks for referrals, one will get them!

Just recently a colleague of mine and I sat down at a popular gourmet hamburger place for lunch. We arrived there around eleven in the morning, and yes, we were starving! We began to look around at all of the potential opportunities within the establishment. Our server took our drink order, and then soon after, we struck up a conversation with her. She appeared to be very busy and stressed out. It was evident that she was in charge of a large section of the restaurant, including the bar. She then took our order and came back a few minutes later to refill our drinks. By the way, we were thirsty too! When she came back with our drinks, we asked her how long she had worked at the restaurant and if she had any vacation plans for the upcoming summer. Her eyes lit up as she told us she was leaving for Mexico the following week with her friend. Once our food arrived, we asked our server to send the general manager over to our table. At this point it was no problem. Can you imagine if we had sat down and our first request was, "We are here to speak to the general manager"? The server probably would have thought, *I haven't even served them yet and they already have a complaint?* It is so important to make everyone feel valued and treat them the same, from the first person you say hello to and to the last one you see when you leave. Soon after our request was granted, the general manager, Mark, arrived at our table.

We told him we were with the bank and then began small talk with him as well. After this we started to tell him that our bank had partnered with his company to give his employees the same benefits that we receive as bank employees. We mentioned to him that this program would even help with retention and encourage direct deposit participation. The final point of the conversation was the free gift of money to his employees for enrolling in our bank program. We talked about the program even more, and at the end of our visit we had an appointment to present this program at his all employees at a meeting the following Saturday.

In looking closely at all three of the stories, there is a common theme. Not once was the introduction leading with product. You will be able to sell product once you have first established a relationship and clients know you as a person. Chances are they know what you do for a living because you tell them your name and the company you represent. In two of the three stories I was able to pick up on small clues that led to opportunities in the same visit. The first clue was the client's jacket in relation to his current employer. In the second story, the clue was the gold necklace with the power lifter attached to it. You will be able to tell a lot about your clients by making silent observations and then asking sincere questions to learn more about them. By doing so you will show your clients that you truly want to form a partnership with them. In the third illustration we first began to establish rapport with our server and then with the decision maker. When you are around your coworkers at the bank, practice small talk with them and then transition in to product. While having a personal conversation you will pick up a small clue that you can tie product into second hand. Every single person you see, whether inside the bank or out of the bank, is an opportunity. Even ask the business partners you work with. You would be surprised at the opportunities you can discover, especially surrounding employees who have just come aboard the company. When you know your client and they feel valued, they will continue to come back to give you more business. Imagine if you were a customer and you walked into the bank and the first person that greeted you said, "Hi, I'm Travis. Have you heard about our new money market promo?" The client would most likely say, "I came here to do a transaction. Don't bother me." You haven't shown them that you care about them. You are showing them right away you want to sell them something. You are also making known to them that you only care about making a commission. Don't get me wrong; making additional money is important. They don't know who you are. They just came in to do a transaction. By knowing your clients, you will not be a transaction banker but a relationship banker. Keep shooting for the goal of having meaningful conversations with your prospects and clients and the sales will follow. When you truly care about your clients, you will not think about your commissions, but you will think about helping and looking out for them. Do what is ethical for the customers and you will know them on a much deeper level.

USE IT AND YOU WILL SELL IT

How many times have you gone to buy a car and had the salesperson offer to go for a test drive with you? Imagine a test drive where the conversation is almost nonexistent. You are in the driver's seat, and the salesperson is truly along for the ride. You take the car around corners at high speeds. You may even test the brakes over a wet spot in the road. On the stereo you notice your favorite station is surrounded by neon buttons all around the dash board. The car amazes you as you finish your test drive. At the end you hand the keys over and tell the salesman, "Thank you for the ride."

In banking our customers are in the driver's seat. They want to know the latest technology and how to use it. They want to know the most convenient ways to bank online and do transactions from remote places. As a salesperson, we need to know how our products work, and that includes using them ourselves. We can use the competition's online banking and debit cards as much as we like. Sometimes it isn't convenient to switch everything over to the current bank where we are employed. Keep in mind that not everyone's systems are identical. That is what makes each bank so different. Do you think that when we not only know but also use our own products at work we will better understand and sell more of them? When a customer asks which credit card is the best one to choose from or which account they would most likely benefit from, how wonderful would it be to share our own story with them or the experiences that we have learned from by using our own products? Do you think that when we use our own products we sell we will also capture more referrals from our customers? Overall it is difficult to be passionate about something you have never used.

A few months ago one of the bankers at the branch where I worked came to me and said, "I am really struggling with selling our online banking program. Can you help me out?" The first question that I asked him was, "Sal, do you use it yourself?" He looked down at the floor and sighed for a minute and said, "I don't." Guess what happened in the next ten minutes? He sat at my desk, and I enrolled him in our online banking program. Over the next few weeks his online banking enrollments tripled because he believed in the products that he sold. He not only believed in them but he was also able to explain to his clients the benefits and features of using them. Most importantly, he created value for his clients from his own firsthand experiences.

I am sure most of us have done what is about to happen next. Our clients come in and ask to sit down and consult with us about a problem they have been having with one of the services they are using. The specific problem is that the new debit card they ordered does not have their existing reward points on it. This is one of the big reasons they choose to bank with you. Just imagine your clients' response if you told them, "I have no clue why they didn't transfer over." Maybe some of us do that already. I can assure you that this will not build or deepen the client relationship. However, if you politely explain to them why they lost their reward points and offer them a solution, that will fix the problem immediately. Right then you just created value and deepened your relationship with your client. In this scenario you didn't sell them a product or service, but you gave them infinite insight into the problem they were having. You acted as a trusted advisor.

Let me illustrate another example using the power of three. The three individuals represent a banker, client, and a newly referred client. When you use a product personally that you feel passionate about, it shows in the way your client perceives you. It shows in the tone of your voice in conversations with your client. Now your client is sold on the product that you feel passionate about. That positive energy passes through to your client. In turn, when the client is with his or her friends and family, he or she begins to tell them about the products he or she uses. The client not only recommends the bank you work for but you a trusted advisor.

Begin today to enroll in as many products and services as your bank has to offer. I can promise that as you do so, your sales will increase!

The Power of
Persuasion

In order to know how you stack up against the competition you must first shop them. Go in to your local competitor and find out what specials they are offering. See how the banker treats you and what products he recommends for you. Take mental notes on how long before the employees greet you and how long you have to wait before you are served. Are the employees chatting with each other and totally oblivious that a potential client just walked in the door? Be sure to collect any pamphlets or brochures when you visit them. At the bank where I work, it is suggested that one of the bankers shops the competition every week. We all know we work in a very competitive and changing industry. These shops are crucial in trying to persuade clients to bank with us. The competition shops also allow you to make better recommendations for your clients. Do not ever talk bad about the competition around you when you are with your client. Imagine, if you will, that today one of your clients comes into your office to ask about your current money market rates. You go over the rates together, and at the end of the conversation your client looks up with a sigh and says, "Is that all you are paying on your money markets?" Your response is yes. The client says he or she is just beginning to shop around for the highest money market rate, and you are the first stop. Your response is dramatic. "I can't believe you want to go and spend all of that time looking for a better rate. Hold on, I will be right back. I have something that will save you a lot of time." On the back wall behind the teller line at your bank is a magical list updated weekly of the current competition's bank rates. You take the sheet off of the wall and go over the rates with your client. What should you do next in the sales process?

Somewhere in your office should be your financial calculator to quote how much the money markets will pay them. You begin to plug in their investment amount of $10,000 dollars and show them how much they will earn with each bank. Typically the savings is not substantial by going to the next bank. Keep in mind you already did the shopping for them at no extra charge. You will also call them with any new promotions that your bank is currently offering. You truly are doing what is right for your client. Will the competition let their client know when the newest promotion is out? The answer is probably not. Will the client walk when you show them that the relationship you have is worth a $20-dollar deficit? Let's hope this is not the case.

For the last seven years I have used the same loan officer to do my mortgage loans. Is he persuasive? Yes, probably the most persuasive person I have ever met! What makes him so persuasive? I remember the first mortgage I applied for with him. My mother referred me to him because she has for the last seventeen years worked with him as a realtor. As you can imagine, I was nervous yet excited at the opportunity of being a first-time homeowner. I called him and set up an appointment to meet with him. At the first appointment he asked me several financial related questions, but first he talked to me like I was part of his family. He got to know me on a personal level by asking me about my hobbies and interests. I mentioned to him that I would be going on a vacation the following week. When I returned, he asked me how my vacation was. The phone number he gave me was his direct line. Yes, his personal cell phone. By all means, I am not recommending you to give out your cell phone number. At times for those special clients you may need to give them that undivided attention. We started the loan application together, and he made me feel comfortable about the application process. I let him know the purchase price of the house I was going to buy. He in turn figured out the monthly payment. You might be saying that is no big deal. But wait, he sends me a postcard every time a new promotion comes out. I can call him anytime I want, and he picks up his phone any day of the week. Most importantly, I can call him with any loan amount, and he will figure out the monthly payment over the phone with me. Over the years I have received plenty as have you junk mail about saving money on your mortgage by introductory mortgage rates. When you call these people do you speak to a live person, do they calculate the payments for you on the initial call and each call thereafter? Most of the time you will never meet these people in person to do your loans. I don't think I would change loan officers if the rate the competition was offering was 2 percent! You may think I am kidding, but I am not. Do the math for your clients, and help them see what they will be able to earn or save. Listen in conversations for any upcoming events they have going on in their lives. Upon their return to your office, follow up with them by asking how their last vacation went. You will be surprised, as I have been, at the expression and excitement they will have on their faces. They found an advisor who was really listening and cares about them as a person. I will talk more about listening toward the end of this chapter. You have the expertise and the tools to execute! They will see you as a valuable banker and different than the competition.

Have you ever started your new job and been really excited to learn what products and services the bank has to offer? Have you known some of your coworkers or business partners who know the products they sell like it is second nature? By knowing the products you sell you will help you leverage the right product for your clients' needs. When you can keep up with the current and latest products, you will be able to time your client's needs as well.

One afternoon I went to see my doctor for pain that I was having at the bottom of my foot. When I got to the doctor's office, I signed in and patiently waited in the lobby until my name was called. I went into one of the medical rooms and waited for the nurse to arrive. About fifteen minutes later she came in. The first question that she asked was, "Mr. Hunter, what brings you in to the doctor today?" I began to describe the discomfort I was feeling at the bottom of my foot. The nurse continued to ask a series of questions. Shortly thereafter the nurse left the room and in came my doctor. He confirmed the answers that I had given to the nurse regarding her questions. What happens next is very important. Because the doctor knew the symptoms and even what the solution or product was, he then able to make a recommendation.

What good will it do to diagnose our clients, as financial doctors, if we cannot prescribe the right product for them? When we have all of the necessary information by doing a complete profile, then we can make the right recommendation. By having the information from clients we can begin to persuade them to buy our products but only when we know the products that we can provide for them. The word recommendation is a word that is very persuasive. It is a word that makes you seem as their trusted advisor—someone who has been in their shoes and can relate to what is best for them.

The next and final important sales tip when persuading a client to buy something from you is to listen. The best salespeople I know are excellent listeners. Therefore, they are also excellent closers. The most important word you will hear your clients say is their own names. Please use their names often and sincerely. Do you know how much information you can gather by asking open-ended questions and then intently listening? You will be able to find out where they work, personal life, kids, other assets, and many other opportunities. In following appointments, you will be able to target certain hot buttons to touch on. Whenever the closing question is asked, remain silent and do not say another word. Pay close attention to the nonverbal language. Watch their facial expressions when you make recommendations for them. Hone in on the topics that really grab their attention. When clients tell you what they need, restate back to them what they need. This will also show that you are listening to what their needs are. Being able to communicate openly and effectively requires excellent listening skills. By listening, it also shows the client that you really care and that they have your undivided attention. Make your clients feel like they are the only ones in the bank. They want to feel valuable, and they depend on you to look out for them.

Last month I walked into a local pharmacy that participates in our bank at work program. For some reason or another I decided to walk straight back to the pharmacy area, where I was greeted by two pharmacists. I introduced myself to them and began asking them questions pertaining to pharmacy school and how they liked their current positions as pharmacists. The conversation lasted a few minutes, and then I told them what I could offer to them. I spoke about how our bank had partnered up with their company and that I would not be doing my job had I not introduced them to this program. The one pharmacist mentioned that she was not interested and began to start working again. The second one listened intently as I changed my tone of voice to a quieter tone to cover the most important parts of the program. I then pulled out a rewards catalog and sold her on the value of the program and most importantly how she would be rewarded by banking with us. She then began to fill out the quick application at the pharmacy counter. What happened then was next to being miraculous. The pharmacist who said no and was happy with her current bank glanced at me and said, "Can I have the same benefits that she receives?" I replied, "Of course you can," as I gently slid the quick application toward her, laid down my pen, and said, "You will love this program!" You see, when prospects see value, they are more likely to be persuaded by what you say or request them to do. At first she was not interested at all until her friend saw and heard how valuable the program is and that she could benefit greatly by using this banking program. As you see from this scenario, the impact you have on one client can have an impact on another. When they are sold and see the value, it can persuade others to join your portfolio. If your bank does not have the same branding or market share as the largest banks, you will not be able to survive on walk-in business. Having good persuasion skills is an absolutely essential tool in surviving in the marketplace. Think back to how you were persuaded to come aboard your current employer. Did the salary help in making your decision? Was it the medical benefits package and retirement plans? You left your old company without knowing what the other side of the pasture looked like. You were persuaded by something or a concept to make the switch to where you are now.

Our clients are persuaded in a similar fashion. We need to discover what their hot buttons are by asking pertinent questions. I know for a fact I can go back and call certain clients because I know where they see value. When you are filling out your profiles for the first time and thereafter, take specific notes on what your clients like and dislike. By knowing this you will be able to better persuade them into buying what right for them. Remember, in the process of persuasion, it boils down to knowing the competition, calculations, listening, adding value, and asking for the business.

Follow Up

Clients like to be called even though you may have not resolved their issue yet. They like it when you call just to give them an update on the status of their problem. Just recently a client needed me to order about eight months of statements. The very next day the statements came, and there was one month worth of bank statements. The weekend came, and my client came in to do a transaction at the teller line. I walked up to him at the teller line and reported to him the status for the whereabouts of his statements. Even though I didn't have all of his statements yet, he appreciated that I at least gave him an update. Imagine, if you will, your closet friends and family. Think back to how you felt when they may not have delivered on their promises. How did it make you feel inside? Your clients will feel the same way. They will feel like they are not important and they are truly just another number that decided to bank with you. I have literally witnessed an incident where a banker did not follow up with his client on a certain issue. If the issue would have been resolved in a timely manner by the banker, the issue would not have gone up the ladder to the banker's boss. When follow up is properly executed, it makes things easier for the whole branch. After all, you did promise your client you would call him or her back and make sure the issue would be resolved. Even when you do not have the answer, do not wait days to give clients a call. Your clients will appreciate you calling them before it is resolved because it shows them that you are working on their case. The time of our clients is very sensitive, and so is ours. We can make life easier for everyone by using the proper follow-up skills. In the next segment of this chapter I will discuss the importance of following up and how it equates to more sales.

Have you ever heard your clients say they have many different choices of where they could bank? They know about these choices because other banks have followed up with them through different methods such as marketing and sales calls or visits. If we are not following up with our clients and prospects, I can guarantee that another banker from another bank will. Some other banker is following up more to gain your clients' business. The point is not to become annoying but to let them know we are there to win their business. So many times the sale is made and the banker has worked so hard to make the sale. What happens after the sale is made? The client does not hear from the banker maybe for months or not at all. One of my favorite questions to ask prospects when competing for their business is, "When was the last time your banker spoke with you?" The more that you follow up, the greater your chances of making a sale happen. You may come in at the perfect time when the competitor has made a mistake and you can capitalize on the error. Go through all of your existing files and make the thirty-, sixty-, and ninety-day touches to your client. Make sure the client has everything he or she needs. Doing this alone will help to deepen the relationship. It will also help you to time your client's needs by anticipating them through your regular contacts with him or her. Think of all of the opportunities you are missing by not having regular contact with your clients. The bottom line is that clients will leave another bank because they did not have a relationship with anyone there. They could have, and it isn't up to them—it is up to you!

While having a conversation with a business prospect, I posed the question, "What is most important to you when choosing a bank?" He answered, "For me it is about convenience and service." If we don't follow up with our clients, we are not servicing them. Part of excellent customer service is delivering on our follow through and executing. When we take care of our clients, they will take care of us!

This year one of my clients who I have been able to retain for the last five years came into the bank with his friend. He had always been one of my best deposit customers. His favorite product seemed to be certificates of deposit. This particular visit he was not interested in cds but business banking. Since the first day I met him I had been working hard to get his business account and business loans. His response was exactly the same each time…I have been with my bank for fifteen years now and have everything with them, and I don't want to switch because it will become such a hassle. Just the previous year he had sold his business to his daughter. His daughter continued to use the same bank until…my client informed me that his daughter was looking to switch banks due to one of her bankers no longer being with the company. He said, "Besides, you are the only banker who really competes for our business." When we can show our clients that we will actually work for their business, I can promise you that they will begin to respect you for it. Do the things that the competition does not do. I said to him, "Not only will I be around for the business during the sales process but after the sale is complete as well." By constantly reaching out and continually asking for the business, I was now able to make the sale. As with my client I have known personally the last five years, it wasn't easy to obtain his business. Our potential clients will test us often during the sales cycle. I definitely would want all of their existing relationship from another bank. But they will give us one piece at a time. They are testing us to see if we will give them the attention and service that they need. Somehow along the path they have been sold by someone who has not even remotely delivered on their promise. The sale is made, and then they never hear from their banker again. When there is a problem, the banker could care less. All that matters is the commission he or she made when the product was sold. Let's not be one of these types of bankers, because it will send a message to our clients that we don't care about them and we don't want more business. When we can take care of the one piece of their portfolio that they give to us and manage it well, they will then trust us and like us enough to give us more business.

I can give you a perfect example of this. One of my first clients at the bank that I work for now was referred to me by the private client group of the bank. This customer was looking for a long-term certificate of deposit manager's special. I was able to open her account for her. This product didn't expire for over a year, so why would I need to keep in touch with her until it came due? Not to mention, the cd was a jumbo cd. A month later I gave her a follow up phone call to touch base with her. I started with small talk and then transitioned into banking. I talked to her about our newest promotion, which happened to be a money market savings promotion. At this point I had a good relationship with my client, and I was able to ask for more business. Another month and then two months went by and I gave her a call and talked to her and then talked about another promotion we were having on checking accounts, especially interest bearing. She then decided to open up a checking account with me and closed her existing one from her other bank. You may not get the whole relationship at once, but let your prospects know they should try you out and see how it goes. For our clients, it is much easier to switch one account to another bank than it is to change five accounts over to another bank.

As one of the top sales representatives, I am always selling at work and even outside of work. About two months ago I was at the gas station filling up my gas tank. After I was done, I went into the gas station to pay for the fuel. I couldn't help but ask where the front desk cashier banked. His reply was very bold, and he seemed annoyed as he gave his answer.

Whether you are following up on the service side or the sales side, both are equally important. You cannot have one or the other to be successful in this business. You must work on becoming excellent at following up on the service and the sales side. Business is won and lost due to follow up. I love the quote, "What it takes to be number one," by Vince Lombardi. I will paraphrase it. He says you don't become number one by doing things right once in a while. You become number one by doing things right all of the time. The best bankers in the country don't follow up with their clients once in a while or when they feel like it. They follow up with them constantly because they know their clients need change frequently. They know the importance of keeping and delivering on their promises. The reason they know is because they have followed up with their clients. If you take away one thing from this book, let it be this…. When it comes to follow up, it will be the difference between you and the banker next door. It will be the difference between being a superstar or just an average banker. You are reading this book because you want to be recognized as one of the elite bankers in your field!

THE SIXTH CENTS

I want to spend some time talking about the value of partnerships. There are three different types of partnerships. The partnerships I am referring to are a partnership with your business partners, a partnership with a mentor within the bank, and lastly, a partnership with a business in the community. When you are able to cultivate and develop these three partnerships, you will have a powerful combination. Even with all the talent in the world, these partnerships will not operate effectively unless there is one ingredient—chemistry.

The first partnership I would like to discuss is that of working with banking partners. Some examples of this may include but are not limited to office managers, branch managers, business banking officers, merchant service representatives, treasury management, private client group, district managers, and so forth. One of the first things you should do is become familiar with how these partners operate and what products and services they can provide. In doing so, you will be able to discover hidden opportunities through profiling with your clients. Throughout this past year our branch has struggled with investments. Our revenue number had remained at zero for the better half of this year. Then, recently we had our partner in the investment division come out and do some training. He spent a few hours at the branch dividing the sales team into two groups and in detail went through how he could help us find additional investment opportunities. The partnership became stronger as he came out to the branch to do training. As a result of a face-to-face visit and training, the branch began to profile deeper and look for investment opportunities. Also, there began to be appointments set around investments. As a result of these appointments, the revenue no longer was zero. By having the investment partner come out, it created an awareness and almost so far to say accountability within the branch. Even if he was the greatest investment salesman in the world, it wouldn't matter if there wasn't chemistry between him and the sales team. By developing a strong partner relationship, everyone benefits, from the banker to the partner to the branch to the bank to the shareholder. Also keep in the mind that some areas of the bank you may want to move into one day. By establishing and referring business to a specific partner, you may help yourself advance your career, especially if what they are doing is of interest to you. Be sure to set clear expectations with your partners. Can you see why partnerships, especially internally, are so important?

The next partnership I would like to talk about is the partnership with someone in the bank who does your job really well. The best teachers are those who have gone before and experienced the unknown. I remember many years ago selling air time for a local radio station. The top sales representative could sell anything. I remember going to appointments with him and listening to what he would say on the initial visit. He had this awesome ability to listen and be silent and then make the sale. I learned a lot from him. I would encourage you to spend a day or a few days with that particular individual who does your position extremely well. Be sure to take notes and even mention current situations that are happening in your workplace. Ask him or her for advice with any common objections that you are faced with when prospecting or cold calling. He or she has probably dealt with similar objections before and knows how to remove them. By your willingness to ask him or her questions, it shows that you have a desire or passion to be successful. Chances are he or she probably asked someone when he or she was just starting out, "How do I do this, or what do I say when this happens?" Once you receive advice, be sure to keep in touch with your mentor and let him or her know how things went with a particular client or prospect. It may even be beneficial to hold a conference call weekly or every other week to share some best practices together or as a group.

The last partnership I would like to inform you about is partnerships within the community. If your bank offers bank at work programs or community banking, be sure to get involved in it. The reason I say this is because the opportunities are endless. When you are out prospecting, there are many opportunities that you can look for. Ask to speak with the human resource directors. They are usually the individuals who decide to allow you to come in and offer your programs to their employees. The reason these programs are so effective is because they add value to what the employees are currently being offered by their employer. You won't feel like you are selling anything but providing a service to them and adding value. Just imagine how great it will feel when you are driving to work or on your day off you pass one of these companies and start to think of how many people's lives you made easier by offering these benefits. This is also an incredible way to generate referrals quickly. Most employees do have a best friend at work. When they are satisfied with your services, they will most likely refer you to one of their friends or coworkers. By effectively becoming involved in the community, you become more than a banker; you become an advocate for the community in which you work. By partnering in the community, word about you and your bank will spread faster than having a walk-in customer come in and open an account. You may even want to take your programs to the local park district, the mayor's office, the fire department, and the police station. By doing this, you are truly making a difference in the community in which you work and possibly live. Your goal should be to be an advocate in all three of the partnerships that we have discussed in this chapter. When we do this, we are executing the Sixth Cents.

We have covered a few things around the three different types of partnerships we discover in retail banking. All three partnerships require the sixth sense of chemistry to be successful.

CONCLUSION

Throughout this book we have touched on some very important sales tips. You have discovered and added some takeaways to what you already possess, from why customers bank where they bank to the utmost importance of following up with your clients. While reading this book you have seen real-life success stories as a result of applying these principles with prospects and clients. You have begun to understand that clients do have a choice of who they will choose as their banker. By finishing this book, it is only the beginning with a bright future ahead for you. Even the smallest teachings not proclaimed in the chapter headings, like noticing nonverbal clues about your prospects and clients, is very important in getting to know them. Notice how they will also ask you questions about things they may observe on your desk and in your office. The ideas taught in this book are simply the fundamentals of becoming a successful banker. Take the greatest athletes, businessmen, and leaders of the world for example. They have all mastered and use the fundamentals daily in their own lives. You too will rise to the top as you master the fundamentals in this book. These truly are sales tips you can bank on!

ABOUT THE AUTHOR

Todd Stephen Hunter has held positions in banking from customer service, to relationship banker, office manager, and presently a business banker. Prior to his banking career, Todd has over 9 years of outside sales experience, consistently performing in the top percentile ranking amongst his peers at a nationally known bank in the Chicago market.

Todd proudly presents Sales Tips You Can Bank On!